~A BINGO BOOK~

Inventors and Inventions Bingo Book

COMPLETE BINGO GAME IN A BOOK

Written by Rebecca Stark
Educational Books 'n' Bingo

ISBN 978-0-87386-425-1

Educational Books 'n' Bingo

Printed in the U.S.A.

INVENTORS AND INVENTIONS BINGO
Directions

INCLUDED:

List of Terms

Templates for Additional Terms and Clues

2 Clues per Term

30 Unique Bingo Cards

Markers

1. **Either cut apart the book or make copies of ALL the sheets. You might want to make an extra copy of the clue sheets to use for introduction and review. Keep the sheets in an envelope for easy reuse.**

2. Cut apart the call cards with terms and clues.

3. Pass out one bingo card per student. There are enough for a class of 30.

4. Pass out markers. You may cut apart the markers included in this book or use any other small items of your choice.

5. Decide whether or not you will require the entire card to be filled. Requiring the entire card to be filled provides a better review. However, if you have a short time to fill, you may prefer to have them do the just the border or some other format. Tell the class before you begin what is required.

6. There are 50 topics. Read the list before you begin. If there are any topics that have not been covered in class, you may want to read to the students the topic and clues before you begin.

7. There is a blank space in the middle of each card. You can instruct the students to use it as a free space or you can write in answers to cover topics not included. Of course, in this case you would create your own clues. (Templates provided.)

8. Shuffle the cards and place them in a pile. Two or three clues are provided for each topic. If you plan to play the game with the same group more than once, you might want to choose a different clue for each game. If not, you may choose to use more than one clue.

9. Be sure to keep the cards you have used for the present game in a separate pile. When a student calls, "Bingo," he or she will have to verify that the correct answers are on his or her card AND that the markers were placed in response to the proper questions. Pull out the cards that are on the student's card keeping them in the order they were used in the game. Read each clue as it was given and ask the student to identify the correct answer from his or her card.

10. If the student has the correct answers on the card AND has shown that they were marked in response to the *correct questions,* then that student is the winner and the game is over. If the student does not have the correct answers on the card OR he or she marked the answers in response to *the wrong questions,* then the game continues until there is a proper winner.

11. If you want to play again, reshuffle the cards and begin again.

Have fun!

TERMS INCLUDED

adhesive tape

band-aid

Alexander Graham Bell

barbed wire

Betty Nesmith Graham

Clarence Birdseye

László Bíró

Louis Braille

Luther Burbank

George Washington Carver

Willis H. Carrier

Samuel Colt

Jacques Cousteau

Marie Curie

Leonardo da Vinci

John Deere

George Eastman

Thomas Edison

Albert Einstein

Max Factor

Michael Faraday

George W. Ferris

Henry Ford

Benjamin Franklin

Robert Fulton

King C. Gillette

Robert Goddard

Charles Goodyear

George Gould

Johannes Gutenberg

Elias Howe

Anton van Leeuwenhoek

Guglielmo Marconi

John L. Mason

Cyrus McCormick

Samuel Morse

Sir Isaac Newton

Alfred Nobel

Elisha Graves Otis

Louis Pasteur

George Pullman

Erno Rubik

safety pin

Igor Sikorsky

Levi Strauss

Madame C. J. Walker

Eli Whitney

windshield wiper

Stephen Wozniak

Orville and Wilbur Wright

Additional Terms

Choose as many terms as you would like and write them in the squares.
Repeat each as desired. Cut out the squares and randomly distribute them to the
class. Instruct the students to place the square on the center space of their card.

Inventors & Inventions Bingo

Clues for
Additional Terms

Write two clues for each new topic.

_____ 1. 2. 3.	_____ 1. 2. 3.
_____ 1. 2. 3.	_____ 1. 2. 3.
_____ 1. 2. 3.	_____ 1. 2. 3.

Inventors & Inventions Bingo

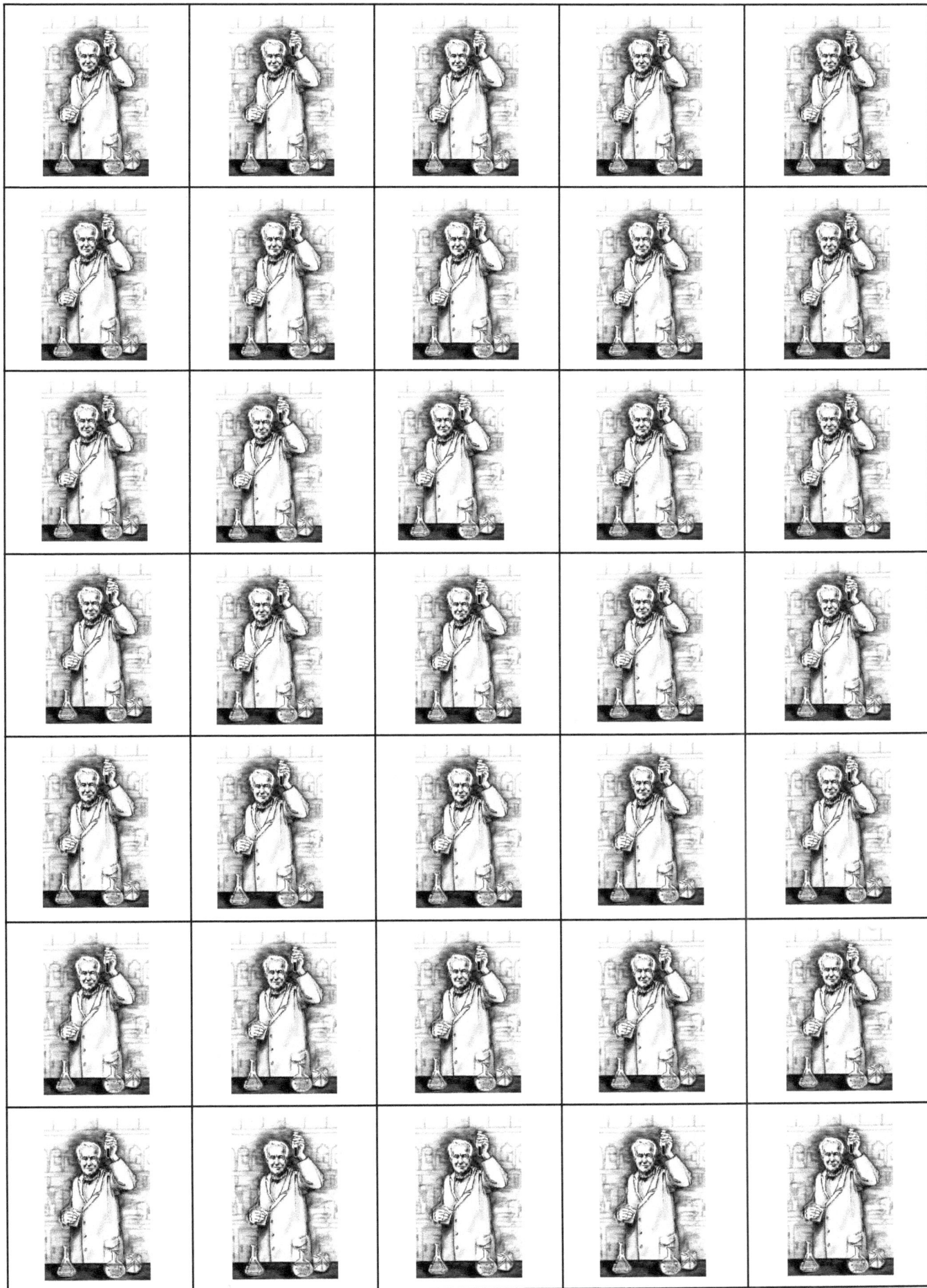

adhesive tape	band-aid
1. Richard Drew, a 3M employee, invented this. 2. Richard Drew, the 3M employee who invented this, also invented masking tape.	1. It was invented by Earle Dickson in 1920 for his wife, who was frequently cutting her hand in the kitchen. 2. Before this invention it was necessary to use separate gauze and adhesive tape in order to protect wounds.
Alexander Graham Bell	**barbed wire**
1. His first words on his telephone were "Mr. Watson—come here—I want to see you." 2. He received a patent for his telephone in March 1876 after a legal battle with Elisha Gray.	1. Joseph Glidden invented a perfected version of this type of fencing in 1874. 2. __ fencing made it easier for ranchers to restrain their cattle. It led to range wars between the cattle ranchers and sheep ranchers.
Betty Nesmith Grahman	**Clarence Birdseye**
1. She invented liquid paper, a product used to cover up mistakes on paper. 2. Her company, founded in 1956, was first called the Mistake Out Company.	1. His method of flash-freezing foods was patented in 1923. 2. He developed a method to make the commercial availability of frozen foods practical.
László Bíró	**Louis Braille**
1. He patented his invention of the ballpoint pen in 1938, 2. In 1945 he sold his patent rights to Marcel Bich. Their low-priced pens made both him and Bich very wealthy.	1. He invented a system of printing that uses raised dots to be read with the fingers. 2. He lived from 1809 to 1852. His system of printing has helped blind people read and write.
Luther Burbank	**George Washington Carver**
1. This American horticulturist developed more than 800 strains and varieties of plants. 2. The Idaho potato was originally named after him. It was introduced to Ireland to combat the blight epidemic.	1. This African American scientist discovered about 300 uses for peanuts and 100's for soybeans, sweet potatoes and pecans. 2. In 1897 he became Director of Agriculture at the Tuskegee Institute.

Inventors & Inventions Bingo

Willis H. Carrier 1. He created the first air conditioning in 1902 when working for the Buffalo Forge Company, but he was not the first to use the term "air conditioning." 2. In 1906 he was given a patent for his "apparatus for treating air."	**Samuel Colt** 1. This 19th-century industrialist received a patent for his revolver in 1836. 2. The weapon he invented was said to have "won the West." Several shots could be fired before reloading.
Jacques Cousteau 1. In 1943 he and Emile Gagnan perfected the aqualung. 2. The aqualung, perfected by him and Emile Gagnan, allowed a diver to stay underwater for hours. It was used to locate mines after World War II.	**Marie Curie** 1. She and her husband were awarded half of the Nobel Prize for Physics in 1903 for their study of spontaneous radiation. (Becquerel got other half.) 2. In 1911 she received a Nobel Prize in Chemistry for her work in radioactivity.
Leonardo da Vinci 1. This Renaissance Man was an artist, astronomer, geologist, mathematician, botanist, engineer, architect and more. 2. Although his ornithopter flying machine was never created, it was the inspiration for modern-day helicopters.	**John Deere** 1. He invented the first steel plow in 1837. 2. This American blacksmith founded a company that became the largest manufacturer of agricultural and construction equipment in the world.
George Eastman 1. He lived from 1854 to 1932 and held many patents in the field o photography. 2. In 1884 he registered the trademark Kodak.	**Thomas Edison** 1. He and his team invented the first practical light bulb in 1879. 2. This great inventor is sometimes called the "Wizard of Menlo Park." He held 1,093 patents.
Albert Einstein 1. His equation—$E=mc^2$—laid the foundation for atomic bomb. He received the 1921 Nobel Prize in Physics. 2. Best known for his theory of relativity, he held several patents, including one for a refrigerator with no moving parts.	**Max Factor** 1. This Polish makeup artist lived from 1877 to 1938. He invented makeup for movie actors that would not crack. 2. He is sometimes called the "Father of Modern Makeup."

Inventors & Inventions Bingo

© Barbara M. Peller

Michael Faraday	**George W. Ferris**
1. In 1831 he discovered electromagnetic induction. His induction ring was the first electric transformer. 2. This British scientist invented the electric motor.	1. This bridge-builder from Pittsburgh, Pennsylvania, invented a ride that is named for him. 2. The ride this engineer designed was a big hit at the World's Columbian Exposition in Chicago in 1893.
Henry Ford	**Benjamin Franklin**
1. He did not invent the assembly line, but he improved it greatly for automobile manufacturing. 2. His Model-T, which was powered by gas, became very popular.	1. He invented the lightning rod after using a key and a kite to show that lightning bolts are electrical currents. 2. His inventions include bifocal glasses, a glass armonica, an odometer and a wood stove.
Robert Fulton	**King C. Gillette**
1. He did not invent the steamboat, but he is credited with making steamboating a commercial success. 2. His steamboat, the *Clermont*, made its first trip from New York City to Albany on August 7, 1807.	1. He did not invent the safety razor, but he did improve it. Production of his improved safety razor began in 1903. 2. His real success came from his invention and marketing of disposable blades for the razor.
Robert Goddard	**Charles Goodyear**
1. In 1914 he received two patents: one for a rocket using liquid fuel and one for a two- or three-stage rocket using solid fuel. 2. He is considered the "Father of Modern Rocket Propulsion."	1. He patented his process for vulcanizing rubber in 1844. 2. His process of vulcanization made rubber waterproof and winter proof. It led to the greater production of rubber products.
George Gould	**Johannes Gutenberg**
1. In 1977 he received his first patent for the laser and was the first to use this term. 2. He wrote down his first thoughts about **l**ight **a**mplification by **s**timulated **e**mission of **r**adiation in 1957.	1. He completed his printing press with replaceable/moveable letters in 1440. 2. His printing press revolutionized the printing of books and led to the rapid development in the sciences, arts and religion.

Inventors & Inventions Bingo

Elias Howe 1. He invented the sewing machine. 2. He sued Isaac Singer for patent infringement because the lockstitch with two spools of thread and an eye-pointed needle was the same. He won the suit.	**Anton van Leeuwenhoek** 1. He invented the first practical microscope. 2. In 1674 he became the first person to see and describe bacteria. He is called the "Father of Microscopy."
Guglielmo Marconi 1. This Italian inventor sent the first successful transatlantic radiotelegraph message in 1902. 2. The experiments carried out by this Italian inventor proved that radio communication was possible.	**John L. Mason** 1. He invented the screw-neck jar in 1838. 2. His easy-to use, re-usable jars made canning popular among American settlers.
Cyrus McCormick 1. He introduced his reaper in 1837 and began to mass manufacture it in a Chicago factory in 1847. 2. His reaper was a horse-drawn machine that harvested wheat.	**Samuel Morse** 1. He invented telegraph wires. 2. He patented the electronic alphabet which is named for him in 1840. He used it to send the first telegraph in 1844. It read, "What hath God wrought?"
Sir Isaac Newton 1. His laws of motion were first published in 1687. 2. Best known for his laws of motion and universal gravitation, he also invented integral calculus and the reflecting telescope.	**Alfred Nobel** 1. He received a patent for dynamite in 1867. He held a total of 355 patents at the time of his death. 2. When he died, he left an endowment fund. It is used every year to award people whose work helps humanity.
Elisha Graves Otis 1. He did not invent the elevator, but he did invent an elevator brake. He demonstrated his invention at the Crystal Palace Exposition in New York in 1854. 2. His invention made elevators safer. It made skyscrapers possible.	**Louis Pasteur** 1. This French chemist & microbiologist is best known for his process of pasteurization. His first test of it was completed in 1862. 2. In addition to inventing pasteurization, he also created the first vaccine for rabies.

Inventors & Inventions Bingo

George Pullman 1. His first railroad "sleeping car" was completed in 1864. 2. He believed that for his sleeper cars to be successful, he had to provide services. He hired former plantation slaves to work on his so-called "Palace Cars."	**Erno Rubik** 1. This Hungarian inventor received a patent for his Magic Cube in1977. 2. When Tibor Laczi decided to invest in his invention, they sold millions of these challenging puzzles.
safety pin 1. Walter Hunt invented it. Before the advent of disposable diapers, this device was commonly used to fasten cloth ones. 2. Hunt's improved one differed from previous ones because it had a clasp and spring action.	**Igor Sikorsky** 1. This Russian aviation designer invented the first successful helicopter in 1939. 2. His helicopters could fly forwards and backwards, up and down, and sideways.
Levi Strauss 1. During the California Gold Rush, he sold pants to miners made from cotton cloth from France, called *serge de Nimes.* The fabric became known as denim. 2. He co-patented the process of putting rivets in the pants for strength.	**Madame C. J. Walker** 1. This African American business-woman lived from 1867 to 1919. 2. Her hair care products for African American women became the basis of a very successful company.
Eli Whitney 1. He invented the cotton gin in 1794. 2. His invention separated seeds, hulls and other unwanted materials from cotton after it has been picked. It revolutionized the American cotton industry.	**windshield wiper** 1. Mary Anderson invented this devise in 1903 after witnessing people open their windows to clean the snow off the windshields. 2. By 1916 this devise invented by Mary Anderson became standard on all cars.
Stephen Wozniak 1. He and Steven Jobs invented the first ready-made personal computer. 2. He and Steven Jobs co-founded Apple Computer, one of the first manufacturers of personal home computers.	**Orville and Wilbur Wright** 1. In 1906 they received a patent for a "flying machine." 2. They made the first airplane flight from Kitty Hawk, North Carolina, on December 17, 1903. They flipped a coin to see who would fly first.

Inventors & Inventions Bingo

Inventors & Inventions Bingo

Albert Einstein	Max Factor	Henry Ford	Eli Whitney	Igor Sikorsky
Luther Burbank	Alexander Graham Bell	Madame C. J. Walker	Charles Goodyear	Michael Faraday
Louis Pasteur	John L. Mason		George W. Ferris	Johannes Gutenberg
windshield wiper	band-aid	George Eastman	Orville and Wilbur Wright	Benjamin Franklin
Robert Fulton	Stephen Wozniak	Willis H. Carrier	adhesive tape	Thomas Edison

Inventors & Inventions Bingo

windshield wiper	Erno Rubik	King C. Gillette	Guglielmo Marconi	Robert Fulton
Benjamin Franklin	Charles Goodyear	Louis Braille	band-aid	Elisha Graves Otis
Samuel Morse	Stephen Wozniak		Samuel Colt	George Eastman
John Deere	Sir Isaac Newton	John L. Mason	Elias Howe	Michael Faraday
Thomas Edison	Madame C. J. Walker	Willis H. Carrier	Luther Burbank	adhesive tape

Inventors & Inventions Bingo

windshield wiper	George Eastman	Charles Goodyear	Orville and Wilbur Wright	Louis Pasteur
Stephen Wozniak	Alexander Graham Bell	Clarence Birdseye	Max Factor	George Gould
band-aid	Madame C. J. Walker		Elisha Graves Otis	barbed wire
John L. Mason	Samuel Morse	Robert Fulton	John Deere	King C. Gillette
adhesive tape	Luther Burbank	Willis H. Carrier	Elias Howe	Henry Ford

Inventors & Inventions Bingo

John L. Mason	Elisha Graves Otis	Henry Ford	Luther Burbank	Robert Fulton
Robert Goddard	Louis Braille	Max Factor	Guglielmo Marconi	Louis Pasteur
George W. Ferris	John Deere		Igor Sikorsky	Orville and Wilbur Wright
George Eastman	Leonardo da Vinci	Madame C. J. Walker	Willis H. Carrier	Clarence Birdseye
adhesive tape	Thomas Edison	Anton van Leeuwenhoek	Marie Curie	Johannes Gutenberg

Inventors & Inventions Bingo

Thomas Edison	Igor Sikorsky	band-aid	Louis Braille	Luther Burbank
Robert Goddard	George Eastman	Clarence Birdseye	Samuel Colt	Alexander Graham Bell
Erno Rubik	Johannes Gutenberg		Jacques Cousteau	Henry Ford
Michael Faraday	Elisha Graves Otis	Albert Einstein	Elias Howe	Marie Curie
Charles Goodyear	Willis H. Carrier	Cyrus McCormick	John L. Mason	George W. Ferris

Inventors & Inventions Bingo: Card No. 5

Inventors & Inventions Bingo

barbed wire	Elisha Graves Otis	King C. Gillette	Erno Rubik	Johannes Gutenberg
Orville and Wilbur Wright	band-aid	Marie Curie	Max Factor	Louis Pasteur
Guglielmo Marconi	Clarence Birdseye		Louis Braille	Samuel Colt
Willis H. Carrier	Robert Fulton	Elias Howe	Anton van Leeuwenhoek	George W. Ferris
Benjamin Franklin	George Eastman	Albert Einstein	Cyrus McCormick	Henry Ford

Inventors & Inventions Bingo

Albert Einstein	Elisha Graves Otis	George Pullman	Jacques Cousteau	Charles Goodyear
Benjamin Franklin	Henry Ford	Stephen Wozniak	Alexander Graham Bell	Robert Goddard
King C. Gillette	Orville and Wilbur Wright		Samuel Colt	Betty Nesmith Grahman
John L. Mason	John Deere	Louis Pasteur	windshield wiper	Samuel Morse
Willis H. Carrier	Luther Burbank	Elias Howe	Anton van Leeuwenhoek	barbed wire

Inventors & Inventions Bingo

George W. Ferris	Elisha Graves Otis	László Bíró	Orville and Wilbur Wright	Betty Nesmith Grahman
Robert Goddard	Erno Rubik	Guglielmo Marconi	Johannes Gutenberg	Louis Braille
Louis Pasteur	Alfred Nobel		Henry Ford	Igor Sikorsky
adhesive tape	John L. Mason	windshield wiper	Marie Curie	John Deere
Madame C. J. Walker	Willis H. Carrier	Anton van Leeuwenhoek	band-aid	Benjamin Franklin

Inventors & Inventions Bingo

Samuel Colt	Charles Goodyear	Stephen Wozniak	Louis Pasteur	Johannes Gutenberg
Marie Curie	Erno Rubik	George W. Ferris	band-aid	Henry Ford
George Gould	Albert Einstein		Alexander Graham Bell	László Bíró
Betty Nesmith Grahman	Thomas Edison	Robert Fulton	Jacques Cousteau	George Pullman
John Deere	Elias Howe	Clarence Birdseye	windshield wiper	Igor Sikorsky

Inventors & Inventions Bingo

windshield wiper	Eli Whitney	Louis Braille	Guglielmo Marconi	Cyrus McCormick
Johannes Gutenberg	Betty Nesmith Grahman	Max Factor	Alexander Graham Bell	Henry Ford
Alfred Nobel	Elisha Graves Otis		Orville and Wilbur Wright	Samuel Morse
Robert Fulton	Michael Faraday	Marie Curie	Elias Howe	George Gould
George Washington Carver	Benjamin Franklin	King C. Gillette	Thomas Edison	George W. Ferris

Inventors & Inventions Bingo

barbed wire	Elisha Graves Otis	band-aid	Marie Curie	Benjamin Franklin
László Bíró	George Gould	Jacques Cousteau	Samuel Colt	Max Factor
Robert Goddard	Erno Rubik		King C. Gillette	Stephen Wozniak
George Washington Carver	Louis Pasteur	Elias Howe	Luther Burbank	windshield wiper
Clarence Birdseye	Willis H. Carrier	Albert Einstein	Anton van Leeuwenhoek	Charles Goodyear

Inventors & Inventions Bingo

Charles Goodyear	Igor Sikorsky	George Gould	Orville and Wilbur Wright	Samuel Colt
Stephen Wozniak	Madame C. J. Walker	Erno Rubik	Anton van Leeuwenhoek	Robert Goddard
Albert Einstein	George Pullman		Johannes Gutenberg	Guglielmo Marconi
Willis H. Carrier	John Deere	Henry Ford	windshield wiper	Alexander Graham Bell
Elisha Graves Otis	László Bíró	Alfred Nobel	Clarence Birdseye	Betty Nesmith Grahman

Inventors & Inventions Bingo: Card No. 12

Inventors & Inventions Bingo

George Washington Carver	Igor Sikorsky	barbed wire	George Gould	Johannes Gutenberg
Erno Rubik	László Bíró	Elisha Graves Otis	Samuel Colt	Samuel Morse
Orville and Wilbur Wright	Louis Braille		Stephen Wozniak	George Pullman
George W. Ferris	Elias Howe	Betty Nesmith Grahman	Alfred Nobel	windshield wiper
Willis H. Carrier	Michael Faraday	Anton van Leeuwenhoek	Albert Einstein	Jacques Cousteau

Inventors & Inventions Bingo

Luther Burbank	Erno Rubik	band-aid	Samuel Colt	George Washington Carver
Betty Nesmith Grahman	Albert Einstein	George Gould	Alexander Graham Bell	Elisha Graves Otis
Marie Curie	Orville and Wilbur Wright		King C. Gillette	Clarence Birdseye
Michael Faraday	Elias Howe	Alfred Nobel	Louis Braille	barbed wire
Willis H. Carrier	Guglielmo Marconi	Samuel Morse	Benjamin Franklin	George W. Ferris

Inventors & Inventions Bingo

Jacques Cousteau	Samuel Colt	band-aid	Charles Goodyear	Orville and Wilbur Wright
barbed wire	Cyrus McCormick	Max Factor	Erno Rubik	Marie Curie
Johannes Gutenberg	Albert Einstein		Louis Pasteur	Henry Ford
Willis H. Carrier	George Gould	László Bíró	Elias Howe	George Washington Carver
Benjamin Franklin	John Deere	Anton van Leeuwenhoek	King C. Gillette	Stephen Wozniak

Inventors & Inventions Bingo

Louis Braille	Levi Strauss	László Bíró	Cyrus McCormick	Sir Isaac Newton
Guglielmo Marconi	Samuel Morse	George Pullman	Robert Goddard	Eli Whitney
George Washington Carver	Igor Sikorsky		Johannes Gutenberg	Stephen Wozniak
John L. Mason	Betty Nesmith Grahman	Willis H. Carrier	Jacques Cousteau	windshield wiper
Marie Curie	George Gould	Anton van Leeuwenhoek	John Deere	Elisha Graves Otis

Inventors & Inventions Bingo

George Washington Carver	safety pin	Leonardo da Vinci	George Gould	Luther Burbank
Jacques Cousteau	Marie Curie	Elias Howe	Orville and Wilbur Wright	George Pullman
Samuel Colt	windshield wiper		Levi Strauss	László Bíró
Thomas Edison	Benjamin Franklin	George W. Ferris	band-aid	Samuel Morse
Robert Fulton	Clarence Birdseye	Charles Goodyear	Eli Whitney	Igor Sikorsky

Inventors & Inventions Bingo

Henry Ford	Alfred Nobel	Betty Nesmith Grahman	Marie Curie	Guglielmo Marconi
Thomas Edison	George Washington Carver	band-aid	Johannes Gutenberg	Clarence Birdseye
Samuel Colt	Samuel Morse		Leonardo da Vinci	Cyrus McCormick
Elisha Graves Otis	Max Factor	Elias Howe	windshield wiper	King C. Gillette
Levi Strauss	George Gould	Robert Fulton	safety pin	barbed wire

Inventors & Inventions Bingo

Johannes Gutenberg	barbed wire	George Gould	László Bíró	Alfred Nobel
Jacques Cousteau	Luther Burbank	Cyrus McCormick	Charles Goodyear	Eli Whitney
safety pin	Orville and Wilbur Wright		Alexander Graham Bell	Thomas Edison
King C. Gillette	Levi Strauss	Robert Fulton	John Deere	Leonardo da Vinci
Louis Pasteur	Sir Isaac Newton	Benjamin Franklin	George W. Ferris	Anton van Leeuwenhoek

Inventors & Inventions Bingo

Alfred Nobel	safety pin	Eli Whitney	George Gould	Alexander Graham Bell
Louis Braille	Stephen Wozniak	Robert Goddard	Robert Fulton	Guglielmo Marconi
Igor Sikorsky	George Pullman		John L. Mason	Max Factor
Thomas Edison	George W. Ferris	adhesive tape	John Deere	Levi Strauss
George Eastman	Madame C. J. Walker	Sir Isaac Newton	windshield wiper	Leonardo da Vinci

Inventors & Inventions Bingo

Jacques Cousteau	barbed wire	Robert Goddard	George Gould	Michael Faraday
Igor Sikorsky	Leonardo da Vinci	Betty Nesmith Grahman	László Bíró	Albert Einstein
Samuel Morse	Benjamin Franklin		safety pin	band-aid
Robert Fulton	Charles Goodyear	Levi Strauss	Thomas Edison	George W. Ferris
John L. Mason	Sir Isaac Newton	Anton van Leeuwenhoek	George Washington Carver	John Deere

Inventors & Inventions Bingo: Card No. 21

Inventors & Inventions Bingo

Louis Pasteur	King C. Gillette	Leonardo da Vinci	Erno Rubik	George Washington Carver
Guglielmo Marconi	Eli Whitney	Henry Ford	László Bíró	Alexander Graham Bell
Betty Nesmith Grahman	Orville and Wilbur Wright		Albert Einstein	George Pullman
Levi Strauss	Thomas Edison	John Deere	Max Factor	Luther Burbank
Sir Isaac Newton	Clarence Birdseye	safety pin	Samuel Morse	Robert Goddard

Inventors & Inventions Bingo

Louis Braille	safety pin	Charles Goodyear	Erno Rubik	Anton van Leeuwenhoek
barbed wire	Alfred Nobel	Benjamin Franklin	Jacques Cousteau	Max Factor
King C. Gillette	George Washington Carver		adhesive tape	Albert Einstein
Samuel Morse	Madame C. J. Walker	Levi Strauss	Clarence Birdseye	John Deere
Michael Faraday	George W. Ferris	Sir Isaac Newton	Robert Fulton	Leonardo da Vinci

Inventors & Inventions Bingo: Card No. 23

Inventors & Inventions Bingo

Louis Braille	Alfred Nobel	Luther Burbank	safety pin	László Bíró
Johannes Gutenberg	Anton van Leeuwenhoek	Robert Goddard	Guglielmo Marconi	Albert Einstein
George Pullman	Cyrus McCormick		George Washington Carver	Samuel Morse
Michael Faraday	adhesive tape	Levi Strauss	Clarence Birdseye	Igor Sikorsky
George Eastman	John L. Mason	Sir Isaac Newton	Eli Whitney	Madame C. J. Walker

Inventors & Inventions Bingo

John L. Mason	Robert Goddard	safety pin	band-aid	Leonardo da Vinci
Max Factor	Michael Faraday	Jacques Cousteau	Louis Braille	Alexander Graham Bell
Igor Sikorsky	László Bíró		adhesive tape	Levi Strauss
Cyrus McCormick	Thomas Edison	Madame C. J. Walker	Sir Isaac Newton	Eli Whitney
Anton van Leeuwenhoek	Luther Burbank	Betty Nesmith Grahman	Marie Curie	George Eastman

Inventors & Inventions Bingo

Leonardo da Vinci	safety pin	adhesive tape	Guglielmo Marconi	Cyrus McCormick
King C. Gillette	Orville and Wilbur Wright	László Bíró	Alfred Nobel	Louis Braille
Michael Faraday	Robert Fulton		Eli Whitney	John L. Mason
George Washington Carver	Erno Rubik	Thomas Edison	Sir Isaac Newton	Levi Strauss
George Pullman	Marie Curie	band-aid	Madame C. J. Walker	George Eastman

Inventors & Inventions Bingo

adhesive tape	Betty Nesmith Grahman	safety pin	Alfred Nobel	Stephen Wozniak
Michael Faraday	King C. Gillette	Jacques Cousteau	Levi Strauss	Alexander Graham Bell
Elias Howe	Madame C. J. Walker		Sir Isaac Newton	John L. Mason
Cyrus McCormick	barbed wire	Robert Goddard	George Eastman	Max Factor
George Washington Carver	Eli Whitney	Leonardo da Vinci	Louis Pasteur	George Pullman

Inventors & Inventions Bingo

Johannes Gutenberg	Alfred Nobel	windshield wiper	safety pin	Betty Nesmith Grahman
Stephen Wozniak	Leonardo da Vinci	adhesive tape	Robert Fulton	Eli Whitney
Madame C. J. Walker	Samuel Morse		Cyrus McCormick	Guglielmo Marconi
George Pullman	Louis Pasteur	Benjamin Franklin	Sir Isaac Newton	Levi Strauss
Erno Rubik	Samuel Colt	George Washington Carver	George Eastman	Michael Faraday

Inventors & Inventions Bingo

Leonardo da Vinci	Alfred Nobel	Cyrus McCormick	Jacques Cousteau	Samuel Colt
Michael Faraday	Robert Fulton	Robert Goddard	George Pullman	Louis Pasteur
Igor Sikorsky	safety pin		Alexander Graham Bell	adhesive tape
Stephen Wozniak	Thomas Edison	Henry Ford	Sir Isaac Newton	Levi Strauss
Louis Braille	László Bíró	George Eastman	barbed wire	Madame C. J. Walker

Inventors & Inventions Bingo

Luther Burbank	safety pin	Guglielmo Marconi	Samuel Colt	Levi Strauss
Max Factor	Cyrus McCormick	King C. Gillette	Eli Whitney	Alexander Graham Bell
George Eastman	Clarence Birdseye		George Pullman	Robert Goddard
Michael Faraday	barbed wire	Alfred Nobel	Sir Isaac Newton	adhesive tape
Thomas Edison	Charles Goodyear	Madame C. J. Walker	Leonardo da Vinci	Henry Ford